Illustrated by Amanda Oleander
www.amandaoleander.com
@AmandaOleander

Written by Grace Smith
www.getgrace.com
@GraceSmithTV

Visit www.getgrace.com/books for additional e-gifts and supportive resources for our readers.

For Patrick and Aurora
Mommy GS

For Benny
Mommy AO

EE + OO are

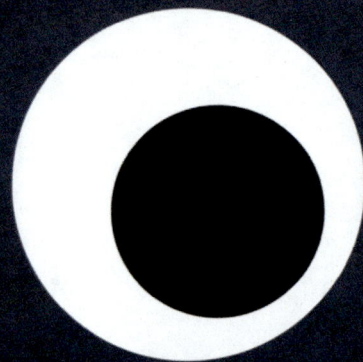

black and white

with brown and blue

and other lovely colors too.

EE and OO are "he" and
"she" and "them"
and "they"
who love adventure
and love to play.

What's the very best
thing about EE and OO?

When put together they sound just like... EEEOOOO... "YOU!"

It's time for You to fill
Your trusty backpack with
all of Your adventure gear.
Your transformation isn't
far away. it's very. very near.

Tonight's adventure is
the adventure of....

Sleep!!

Now take a deep breath
and close Your eyes...
This adventure happens
inside Your mind!

Counting down
verrrryyy slooooowly now...

5... You are feeling sleepier and sleepier.

4... You are going deepier and deepier.

3... You are smiling happier and happier.

2... You are oh so happily sleepier deepier.

1... Your sleepytime adventure begins now...

With Your eyes still closed,
imagine a color You love
flowing in through
the top of Your head,
through Your body, and
out Your toes...

You notice now
You are becoming a sleepy head.
and I wonder how much sleepier
You'll feel by the end...

You love to dream
the happiest dreams
about pink lions who
whoosh by in tophats...

Who bathe in fizzy
lavender streams.
and eat blueberries
with magical elephants!

You're feeling sleepier already. You're breathing slowly with Your tummy. You're starting to yawwwwn. You're ready for the night night song!

"Night night. sleep tight.
There's no need to cry.
You're dreaming already.
snuggly. warm. and dry...

Night night. sleep tight.
There's no need to try.
You're dreaming already.
snuggly. warm. and dry...

Night night. sleep tight.
There's no need to cry.
You're dreaming already.
snuggly. warm. and dry!"

The adventure of You will continue now in Your dreams..
5...4... 3... 2... 1...

The end...
Night night!

Resources

Help your little ones get the most out of their adventure!
Tips and bonus resources for Parents and Caregivers:

This book has been written to uniquely support an easy and calm bedtime experience utilizing the power of the theta brainwave state. The theta brainwave state is more relaxed than daydreaming but more conscious and alert than sleep; it's right in the middle of the two. It is a place where you have direct access to your creativity and problem solving abilities, where you bypass critical factors of the mind and where you can directly upgrade your subconscious beliefs. This is the state that Grace Smith expertly guides her hypnotherapy clients into so that they can rewrite subconscious beliefs that aren't serving them and visualize what they want instead. For example, to remove fears about flying and imagine a safe happy flight instead of one filled with dread or anxiety.

While most adults spend the vast majority of their time in a stressed out beta brainwave state, children under the age of 7 are more commonly than not already in the theta brainwave, which explains their amazing creativity and the way they soak up everything around them like a sponge. Unfortunately their subconscious minds do not come with a helpful filter and so they are soaking up the good and the unhelpful in equal measure.

This book will help tip the scales in the direction of the good. You'll notice some unique choices in the book and even a made up word or two, like "deepier", to help them easily access the theta state and, by extension, a relaxed relationship with bedtime.

Some children will fall asleep the first time you read this book and most children will need to hear this book for a few nights in a row before those new neural pathways have formed enough to associate this book with the act of gently falling asleep.

We recommend you read slowly and speak as calmly as you want your child to feel.

To help your little ones get the most of their Adventure of Sleep, we've created even more free resources that are available to you on line! Find coloring pages, a recording of Grace Smith reading the book for your children in her world renowned hypnotherapist voice, a short video for parents and caregivers on how to read the book aloud in the most effective way, and more at GetGrace.com/Books

Grace Smith wrote **The Adventure of Sleep** to help her little ones get to sleep faster and easier. When she shared it with her dear friend Amanda to see if she would be interested in illustrating the book, Amanda let her know she fell fast asleep after reading it for the first time and took a deep four hour nap ... she was sold! Grace is a Wall Street Journal Bestselling author of four hypnotherapy books for adults and is the founder of GetGrace.com, the world's largest resource for hypnotherapy recordings, global zoom-based hypnotherapy sessions and hypnotherapy certification. Grace's work has been featured on tv shows such as Dr. Oz, the Doctors and in publications such as BBC News, the Atlantic, Forbes and dozens more. She and her wonderful husband, Bernardo Feitosa, run GetGrace.com along with raising their beloved human babies, Patrick and Aurora, and three fur babies, Sweets, Zen and Kona, in Vero Beach, Florida.

Amanda Oleander is a Los Angeles based artist. She started drawing at a young age and has since been recognized in publications such as Vanity Fair, Cosmo, USA Today, The Hollywood Reporter, amongst others, as well as on the TEDX stage. Oleander's illustrations are often a reflection of her own journey through life. Most recently Oleander and her husband, Joey Rudman, welcomed their son Benny into the world. **The Adventure of Sleep** quickly became a bed time favorite.

Please Review

We hope you and your little one have
enjoyed reading The Adventure of Sleep!
Reviews are the best way to spread the word
that a book is worth reading (or not).
Please share an honest review on Amazon; we cannot
wait to celebrate your sleepy time success stories with
you!

Love,
Grace and Amanda

Made in the USA
Las Vegas, NV
04 November 2023